The Green Garbage Guide

Effective Techniques for Minimizing Waste

Lucas Flowers

The Green Garbage Guide

This document is geared towards providing exact and reliable information with regards to the topic and issue covered. The publication is sold with the idea that the publisher is not required to render accounting, officially permitted, or otherwise, qualified services. If advice is necessary, legal or professional, a practiced individual in the profession should be ordered.

From a Declaration of Principles which was accepted and approved equally by a Committee of the American Bar Association and a Committee of Publishers and Associations.

The information provided herein is stated to be truthful and consistent, in that any liability, in terms of inattention or otherwise, by any usage or abuse of any policies, processes, or directions contained within is the solitary and utter responsibility of the recipient reader. Under no circumstances will any legal responsibility or blame be held against the publisher for any reparation, damages, or monetary loss due to the information herein, either directly or indirectly.

The information herein is offered for informational purposes solely, and is universal as so. The presentation of the information is without contract or any type of guarantee assurance.

The trademarks that are used are without any consent, and the publication of the trademark is without permission or backing by the trademark owner. All trademarks and brands within this book are for clarifying purposes only and are owned by the owners themselves, not affiliated with this document.

TABLE OF CONTENTS

Chapter 1: The Three Rs: Reduce, Reuse, Recycle

The Hierarchy of Waste Management

Navigating the complexities of waste management requires an understanding of the underlying principles that drive sustainable practices. At the core of these principles lies the concept of the waste management hierarchy—a structured approach that prioritizes methods of managing waste based on their environmental impact. This hierarchy is a strategic framework designed to minimize waste and its associated negative consequences by emphasizing prevention and resource efficiency.

The hierarchy is typically represented as an inverted pyramid, where the most preferred options are positioned at the top, and the least preferred methods are at the bottom. Each level of the hierarchy serves as a guide for decision-making, encouraging individuals, businesses, and policymakers to adopt practices that align with environmental sustainability.

At the pinnacle of the hierarchy is waste prevention, also known as source reduction. This approach focuses on minimizing the generation of waste at its origin, thereby reducing the need for subsequent waste management processes. Prevention is the most effective strategy because it addresses the problem at its source, eliminating unnecessary waste production. Achieving waste prevention can involve designing products with longevity, repairability, and recyclability in mind, as well as encouraging consumer choices that prioritize durability over disposability.

Following prevention is reuse, which involves finding new applications for items that might otherwise be discarded. Reuse extends the lifecycle of products, conserving resources and reducing the demand for new ones. This can be as simple as repurposing containers, donating unwanted goods, or organizing community swap events where individuals exchange items instead of purchasing new ones. Reuse not only conserves materials but also fosters a culture of sustainability and resourcefulness.

Recycling occupies the next tier of the hierarchy, transforming waste materials into new products through processes such as collection, sorting, and processing. While recycling is a more resource-intensive option compared to prevention and reuse, it remains a crucial component of waste management. Proper recycling reduces the volume of waste sent to landfills and conserves natural resources. However, effective recycling requires robust infrastructure, public awareness, and cooperation from various stakeholders to ensure that materials are collected and processed correctly.

Energy recovery follows recycling and involves converting waste materials into usable energy through processes like incineration, anaerobic digestion, or gasification. While energy recovery is less preferable than the aforementioned methods, it presents an opportunity to extract value from waste that cannot be recycled. These processes can generate electricity, heat, or fuel, contributing to energy needs while reducing landfill volumes. It is important to implement these processes with stringent environmental controls to minimize emissions and other potential impacts.

Finally, at the base of the hierarchy is disposal, the least preferred method of waste management. This entails the deposition of waste in landfills or through incineration without energy recovery. While disposal is necessary for waste that cannot be managed through other means, it poses significant environmental challenges, including land use, pollution, and greenhouse gas emissions. Efforts to reduce reliance on disposal are essential to achieving sustainable waste management outcomes.

Understanding the hierarchy of waste management is crucial for making informed decisions that contribute to environmental preservation. By prioritizing prevention and resource efficiency, individuals and organizations can play an active role in reducing waste and its associated impacts. Embracing the hierarchy requires a shift in mindset, moving away from a linear "take-make-dispose" model to a circular approach where resources are continuously cycled back into the economy.

To effectively implement the hierarchy, it is essential to recognize that waste management is a shared responsibility. Collaboration between consumers, businesses, and governments is vital to creating systems that support sustainable practices. Consumers can drive change by making informed choices and advocating for products and services that align with the principles of the hierarchy. Businesses can innovate by designing products for longevity and recyclability, while governments can enact policies that incentivize sustainable practices and provide the necessary infrastructure for waste prevention and recycling.

Education and awareness are key components of successful waste management. By fostering a deeper understanding of the hierarchy and its benefits, individuals and communities can be empowered to take action. Educational programs, workshops, and campaigns can provide valuable insights into how waste management practices can be integrated into daily life, encouraging behavioral changes that support sustainability.

Innovation also plays a crucial role in advancing waste management practices. Technological advancements and research can lead to the development of new materials, processes, and systems that enhance the efficiency and effectiveness of each tier of the hierarchy. For example, advancements in recycling technology can improve the quality and quantity of materials that can be recycled, while innovations in product design can minimize waste generation from the outset.

Moreover, adopting the hierarchy of waste management can have positive economic implications. By reducing waste, businesses can lower costs associated with raw materials, production, and disposal. Recycling and reuse initiatives can create jobs and stimulate economic activity in sectors such as waste collection, processing, and manufacturing. Additionally, energy recovery can contribute to energy security by providing an alternative source of power.

Implementing the hierarchy is not without its challenges. It requires a comprehensive approach that considers social, economic, and environmental factors. Barriers such as lack of infrastructure, limited public awareness, and economic constraints can hinder progress. However, overcoming these challenges is essential to realizing the full potential of sustainable waste management.

The hierarchy of waste management serves as a blueprint for achieving a more sustainable future. By prioritizing waste prevention, reuse, recycling, and energy recovery, society can reduce its environmental footprint and move towards a circular economy. Embracing this framework requires a collective effort, but the rewards are substantial—a healthier planet, resilient communities, and a more sustainable way of living.

Effective Reduction Strategies for Households

Managing household waste effectively begins with understanding the significance of reduction strategies that can significantly contribute to a more sustainable lifestyle. By adopting practical and mindful approaches to waste reduction, individuals can not only minimize their environmental impact but also cultivate a sense of responsibility towards the planet. The journey towards effective waste reduction within a household starts with small, intentional changes that collectively make a substantial difference.

One of the most fundamental strategies is to engage in mindful consumption. This involves being conscious of the items brought into the home, considering their necessity, longevity, and environmental impact. Before purchasing, it's beneficial to ask whether an item is truly needed and whether it will serve a lasting purpose. Embracing minimalism and intentional living can lead to significant waste reduction, as it encourages the acquisition of only what is essential.

Another impactful approach is to focus on reducing single-use products. These items, often used for convenience, contribute significantly to household waste. Transitioning from single-use to reusable alternatives is a straightforward yet powerful way to cut down on waste. For instance, replacing disposable water bottles with a durable, refillable water bottle can prevent countless plastic bottles from entering landfills. Similarly, opting for cloth napkins, reusable shopping bags, and washable cleaning cloths can reduce reliance on disposable counterparts.

Food waste is a pervasive issue in households, yet it presents a valuable opportunity for waste reduction. Meal planning and proper portion control play a crucial role in minimizing food waste. By planning meals in advance and creating shopping lists based on those plans, individuals can avoid over-purchasing and reduce the likelihood of food spoiling before it is used. Additionally, learning to store food properly can extend its shelf life, further preventing waste.

Composting is another effective strategy for managing organic waste. Setting up a simple composting system in the backyard or using a countertop compost bin can turn kitchen scraps and yard waste into nutrient-rich compost. This not only diverts organic waste from landfills but also enriches garden soil, supporting a sustainable cycle of growth. Composting is an empowering practice that connects households with the natural recycling processes of the environment.

In the pursuit of waste reduction, it's essential to consider packaging waste, which often makes up a significant portion of household trash. Opting for products with minimal or recyclable packaging can drastically reduce waste. Buying in bulk is another way to minimize packaging, as it often involves less overall waste per unit of product. Additionally, choosing products packaged in materials that are easily recyclable, such as glass, metal, or certain plastics, supports waste reduction efforts.

Repurposing and repairing items can also extend their lifespan and reduce waste. Before discarding items, consider whether they can be repaired or repurposed for a different use. Simple repair skills, such as sewing, gluing, or fixing basic electronics, can save items from being thrown away prematurely. Creativity plays a significant role in repurposing, as it encourages thinking outside the box to find new uses for old items.

Household waste reduction can further be enhanced by implementing waste segregation practices. By clearly distinguishing between recyclable and non-recyclable waste, and ensuring that recyclables are clean and sorted correctly, households can improve the efficiency of recycling processes. Setting up designated bins for different types of waste streamlines the segregation process and instills a sense of responsibility in all members of the household.

Education and awareness are vital components in fostering a waste-conscious household. Sharing knowledge about the environmental impact of waste and the benefits of reduction strategies can motivate family members to participate actively in waste reduction efforts. Engaging children in waste reduction activities, such as creating art from recyclables or participating in community clean-up events, can instill lifelong values of sustainability and stewardship.

Technology and smart devices can also play a role in waste reduction. Utilizing apps and tools that track food inventory, suggest recipes based on available ingredients, or remind users of expiration dates can help reduce food waste. Smart home systems that optimize energy and water usage contribute to overall resource conservation, aligning with waste reduction goals.

Incorporating these strategies into daily life requires commitment and a willingness to adapt. It's important to recognize that waste reduction is a gradual process, with incremental changes leading to lasting impacts. By integrating these practices into the household routine and reevaluating consumption habits, individuals can create a sustainable living environment that benefits both their immediate surroundings and the broader ecosystem.

Effective waste reduction strategies for households are not just about minimizing waste; they represent a shift towards a more mindful and intentional way of living. By embracing practices that prioritize sustainability and resource conservation, households can significantly reduce their environmental footprint. Each small action contributes to a larger movement towards a more sustainable future, where waste is minimized, resources are valued, and the planet is respected.

Creative Reuse and Upcycling Ideas

The art of creative reuse and upcycling opens a world of possibilities for transforming everyday items into something new and useful, while significantly reducing waste. This approach not only offers environmental benefits but also fosters creativity and innovation. By reimagining the potential of discarded materials, individuals can contribute to a more sustainable future and bring a sense of craftsmanship and personalization into their lives.

One of the most accessible ways to begin upcycling is by repurposing glass containers. Glass jars and bottles, often deemed as waste, can be transformed into functional and decorative items. With a bit of creativity, glass jars can become charming candle holders, planters, or storage containers for kitchen essentials like spices and grains. Painting or etching designs onto the glass adds a personal touch, turning otherwise mundane objects into eye-catching decor.

Fabric scraps and old clothing present another avenue for upcycling. Instead of discarding worn-out garments, consider turning them into something new and stylish. An old t-shirt can be refashioned into a reusable tote bag, while remnants of fabric can become patchwork quilts or colorful cushion covers. Sewing skills are a valuable asset in this endeavor, but even simple no-sew techniques, such as tying knots or using fabric glue, can yield impressive results.

Furniture offers a canvas for larger upcycling projects. Old wooden chairs, tables, or dressers can be given a new lease on life with a fresh coat of paint or a new upholstery. Sanding down and refinishing wooden surfaces can reveal the natural beauty of the material, while adding unique hardware or stenciling patterns can personalize the piece. An old ladder can be repurposed into a bookshelf, and a vintage suitcase can be transformed into a quirky coffee table. The possibilities are only limited by imagination.

For those with a penchant for the industrial aesthetic, metal objects offer intriguing opportunities for upcycling. Discarded pipes, nuts, and bolts can be repurposed into functional fixtures or decorative art. A collection of metal gears, for instance, can be assembled into a striking wall clock, while old bicycle parts can be crafted into a unique lamp. The durability of metal makes it an ideal candidate for projects that require resilience and strength.

Upcycling also extends to paper products, which are abundant in most households. Newspapers, magazines, and old books can be transformed into a variety of items, from handmade greeting cards to intricate paper sculptures. Paper mache is a versatile technique that allows for the creation of decorative bowls, masks, or even furniture. By layering strips of paper with glue, new forms can be molded and painted to create personalized art pieces.

In the realm of technology, outdated electronics might seem like a challenge to upcycle, but they hold untapped potential. An old computer monitor can be converted into a fish tank, while an obsolete smartphone can be repurposed as a digital photo frame. Electronic components such as circuit boards and wires can be used in crafting jewelry or sculptures, adding a modern twist to traditional designs.

The process of creative reuse is not only about giving objects a second life but also about developing a mindset that values resourcefulness and sustainability. It encourages individuals to view waste not as an end but as a beginning, an opportunity to innovate and create. This perspective shift can have a profound impact on how we interact with our environment and consume resources.

Communities can harness the power of upcycling by organizing workshops and events that promote sharing skills and ideas. These gatherings foster collaboration and inspiration, bringing together people with diverse talents and backgrounds. By building networks of like-minded individuals, communities can amplify the impact of upcycling efforts and drive meaningful change on a larger scale.

For those looking to expand their creative horizons, exploring online platforms and social media can provide a wealth of inspiration and tutorials. The global upcycling community is vibrant and active, with countless resources available to guide beginners and seasoned crafters alike. Engaging with this community can spark new ideas and provide valuable insights into innovative techniques and materials.

Businesses and organizations can also play a pivotal role in promoting upcycling by incorporating it into their practices. Offering workshops or selling upcycled products can attract environmentally conscious consumers and set an example for sustainable business operations. By highlighting the environmental benefits and unique qualities of upcycled products, businesses can tap into a growing market of eco-friendly consumers.

The beauty of upcycling lies in its ability to merge sustainability with creativity, offering a fulfilling and impactful way to engage with the world around us. By embracing upcycling, individuals can contribute to reducing waste and conserving resources, all while expressing their creativity in meaningful ways. This approach not only benefits the environment but also enriches lives, fostering a sense of accomplishment and connection to the broader movement towards sustainability.

Recycling Best Practices and Challenges

Recycling is a cornerstone of sustainable waste management, offering a way to conserve resources and reduce landfill waste. However, to truly harness its benefits, it's essential to adopt best practices that enhance the recycling process while navigating the inherent challenges. By understanding the nuances of recycling, individuals and communities can optimize their efforts and contribute to a more sustainable future.

At the heart of effective recycling is the principle of contamination-free sorting. One of the most common challenges faced by recycling programs is the presence of non-recyclable materials in bins designated for recyclables. Contaminants like food residue, plastic bags, or non-recyclable items can compromise entire batches of recyclables, rendering them unusable. To counter this, individuals should familiarize themselves with local recycling guidelines, ensuring that only accepted materials are placed in the recycling bin. Rinsing containers to remove food residue and avoiding the disposal of plastic bags in recycling bins are simple yet impactful steps in maintaining the integrity of recyclable materials.

Understanding the specific materials that can be recycled in a given area is crucial for effective recycling. While some materials like aluminum cans, glass bottles, and certain plastics are commonly recyclable, others may vary based on local facilities and capabilities. Municipalities often provide resources or websites outlining which materials are accepted, and adhering to these guidelines ensures that recycling efforts are not in vain. Moreover, being aware of material types can help in making informed purchasing decisions, favoring products with recyclable packaging.

The concept of "wish-cycling" poses another challenge to recycling efforts. This occurs when individuals place non-recyclable items in recycling bins in the hope that they can be recycled. While well-intentioned, wish-cycling can lead to increased contamination and inefficiencies in the recycling process. It is important to resist the urge to recycle uncertain items and instead consult local guidelines or seek clarification from recycling authorities. By doing so, individuals can ensure that their recycling contributions are beneficial rather than detrimental.

Education and community engagement play vital roles in overcoming recycling challenges. By raising awareness about the importance of proper recycling practices, communities can cultivate a culture of sustainability and shared responsibility. Educational campaigns, workshops, and informational materials can empower individuals with the knowledge needed to recycle effectively. Schools, workplaces, and community centers can serve as platforms for disseminating information and promoting recycling best practices.

For businesses, implementing recycling programs requires a comprehensive approach that involves employee training, clear signage, and convenient access to recycling bins. Encouraging employees to participate in recycling efforts not only contributes to waste reduction but also enhances corporate sustainability goals. Businesses can lead by example, demonstrating their commitment to environmental stewardship and inspiring others to follow suit.

Technological advancements offer promising solutions to some of the challenges associated with recycling. Innovations in recycling technology, such as advanced sorting systems and improved processing methods, have the potential to increase the efficiency and efficacy of recycling programs. For example, optical sorting technology can accurately separate different types of plastics, reducing contamination and improving the quality of recycled materials. Embracing these technologies can enhance recycling outcomes and support the circular economy.

The global nature of recycling presents both opportunities and challenges. International markets for recyclable materials can influence local recycling programs, affecting the demand and value of certain materials. Fluctuations in these markets can impact the feasibility of recycling certain materials, highlighting the importance of developing resilient, localized recycling systems. By fostering partnerships and collaborations across regions, communities can create robust networks that support recycling efforts and adapt to changing market conditions.

Despite the challenges, the benefits of recycling are undeniable. Recycling conserves natural resources, reduces greenhouse gas emissions, and decreases the need for landfill space. By incorporating recycling best practices into daily routines, individuals contribute to a more sustainable environment and support the broader goals of waste management.

Recycling is not just a mechanical process; it is an opportunity to engage with sustainability on a personal level. By taking the time to understand and implement best practices, individuals can make a significant impact on the environment and inspire others to do the same. Through education, innovation, and collaboration, recycling challenges can be overcome, paving the way for a future where resources are used wisely and waste is minimized.

Case Studies of Successful 3Rs Initiatives

Real-world examples can provide valuable insights into how the principles of the three Rs—reduce, reuse, recycle—are being effectively implemented across various contexts. Examining these successful initiatives offers inspiration and practical guidance for individuals and communities striving to adopt sustainable practices.

In Japan, the town of Kamikatsu stands as a beacon of commitment to waste reduction and recycling. Faced with the challenges of limited landfill space and high waste management costs, the town embarked on an ambitious journey towards zero waste. Residents embraced a rigorous sorting system, dividing waste into 45 categories to ensure maximum recyclability. This meticulous approach, coupled with community education and engagement, has led to an impressive recycling rate of over 80%. The success of Kamikatsu illustrates the power of collective action and the importance of community involvement in achieving waste reduction goals.

Closer to home, San Francisco serves as a model of urban sustainability with its comprehensive waste management program. The city's commitment to achieving zero waste by 2020 led to the implementation of policies that prioritize waste prevention and resource recovery. A key component of San Francisco's success is its mandatory composting and recycling program, which requires residents and businesses to separate organic waste from recyclables and landfill-bound materials. The program has been supported by extensive public education campaigns and incentives, resulting in a diversion rate of over 80%. San Francisco's experience highlights the role of policy and regulation in driving large-scale change.

Moving to the corporate sector, the furniture company IKEA has made significant strides in integrating the three Rs into its business model. Recognizing the environmental impact of its products, IKEA launched a circular economy initiative aimed at extending the lifecycle of its furniture. The company introduced a buy-back program, allowing customers to return used furniture for resale or recycling. This initiative not only reduces waste but also aligns with IKEA's goal of becoming climate positive by 2030.

By embracing circularity, IKEA demonstrates how businesses can innovate to reduce their environmental footprint while meeting consumer demands for sustainable options.

In the realm of education, the Eco-Schools program has been instrumental in promoting the three Rs among students worldwide. This international initiative empowers students to take an active role in waste management within their schools, fostering a culture of sustainability from a young age. Participating schools implement waste reduction strategies, such as paper recycling, composting, and waste audits, while integrating environmental education into the curriculum. The program's success is reflected in the positive behavioral changes observed in students, who often carry these sustainable habits into their homes and communities.

A remarkable example of creative reuse can be found in the city of Rotterdam, where the BlueCity project has transformed a former swimming complex into a hub for circular innovation. This collaborative space hosts businesses that focus on upcycling and resource recovery, turning waste streams into valuable products. By fostering a community of like-minded entrepreneurs, BlueCity promotes the exchange of ideas and resources, driving the development of sustainable business models. The initiative showcases the potential of creative reuse to stimulate economic growth while addressing environmental challenges.

The fashion industry, often criticized for its wasteful practices, has also seen successful initiatives aimed at reducing its impact. The clothing brand Patagonia has long championed environmental responsibility, incorporating the three Rs into its operations. Patagonia's Worn Wear program encourages customers to repair and reuse their clothing, offering repair services and guidance on garment care. Additionally, the company uses recycled materials in its products and advocates for sustainable supply chains. Patagonia's commitment to sustainability underscores the importance of ethical business practices and consumer education in driving industry-wide change.

In India, the city of Pune has developed an innovative waste management system that empowers informal waste pickers. The SWaCH cooperative, formed by waste pickers, provides door-to-door waste collection services, promoting recycling and composting at the source. This model not only enhances waste segregation and resource recovery but also improves the livelihoods of waste pickers, who play a crucial role in the recycling chain. By formalizing and supporting the informal waste sector, Pune has achieved significant waste reduction and social benefits, offering a replicable model for other cities.

These case studies demonstrate that successful implementation of the three Rs requires a multifaceted approach that combines policy, education, community engagement, and innovation. Whether at the level of local government, business, or individual action, these initiatives illustrate the transformative potential of sustainable practices. By learning from these examples, individuals and communities can identify strategies that align with their unique circumstances and contribute to a more sustainable future.

The diversity of these initiatives also highlights the adaptability of the three Rs framework, which can be tailored to different contexts and scales. From small towns to global corporations, the principles of reduce, reuse, and recycle offer a roadmap for reducing environmental impact and conserving resources. The success of these initiatives reinforces the notion that every action, no matter how small, contributes to the broader goal of sustainability.

As we reflect on these case studies, it becomes clear that collaboration and commitment are key to driving meaningful change. By working together and sharing knowledge, we can build a more sustainable world where resources are used wisely, waste is minimized, and communities thrive. These stories serve as a testament to the power of human ingenuity and determination in the pursuit of a better future.

Chapter 2: Source Reduction: Preventing Waste at Its Origin

Designing Products for Minimal Waste

Creating products with minimal waste in mind is an essential step towards sustainable production and consumption. This approach focuses on rethinking and redesigning products to ensure they generate the least amount of waste throughout their lifecycle. By prioritizing efficiency and sustainability from the outset, manufacturers can reduce their environmental impact while meeting the growing consumer demand for eco-friendly products.

A fundamental aspect of designing for minimal waste is selecting the right materials. Choosing sustainable, renewable, or recycled materials can significantly reduce the environmental footprint of a product. For instance, bamboo, a rapidly renewable resource, is a popular choice for products ranging from flooring to kitchen utensils. Its fast growth rate and minimal need for pesticides make it an environmentally friendly alternative to traditional materials. Similarly, recycled plastics and metals can be repurposed into new products, conserving resources and reducing landfill waste.

Durability is another crucial factor in minimizing waste. Designing products to last longer reduces the need for frequent replacements and disposal. High-quality materials, robust construction, and timeless design are key elements of durable products. By focusing on longevity, manufacturers can create items that remain functional and desirable over time, reducing the overall demand for new resources. This shift from a disposable mindset to one of durability and repairability is a cornerstone of sustainable design.

Modularity and adaptability are innovative strategies that allow products to evolve with changing needs. By designing products with interchangeable or upgradable components, manufacturers can extend their lifespan and reduce waste. For example, modular furniture systems enable consumers to reconfigure or expand their pieces as their living spaces change. Similarly, electronic devices with easily replaceable parts can be updated or repaired instead of discarded. This approach not only minimizes waste but also offers flexibility and personalization to consumers.

The concept of cradle-to-cradle design emphasizes designing products with the end of their lifecycle in mind. This approach encourages manufacturers to consider how a product can be disassembled, recycled, or safely returned to the environment after its useful life. By planning for the entire lifecycle, designers can create products that contribute to a circular economy, where waste is minimized, and resources are continuously cycled back into production. This holistic perspective fosters innovation and sustainability in product design.

Packaging is an often-overlooked aspect of product design that can contribute significantly to waste. Reducing packaging waste involves selecting materials that are recyclable or biodegradable and minimizing the amount of packaging used. Innovative solutions, such as reusable or returnable packaging systems, can further reduce waste and appeal to environmentally conscious consumers. Additionally, designing packaging that serves a secondary purpose, such as storage or transport, adds value and functionality, reducing the likelihood of it being discarded.

Involving consumers in the design process can lead to more sustainable products. By understanding consumer needs and preferences, designers can create products that align with their values and expectations. Engaging with consumers through surveys, focus groups, or social media can provide valuable insights into how products are used and perceived, informing design decisions that prioritize sustainability. This collaborative approach fosters a sense of ownership and responsibility, encouraging consumers to use products responsibly and for longer periods.

Technological advancements offer new opportunities for designing products with minimal waste. Additive manufacturing, or 3D printing, allows for precise production with minimal material waste. This technology enables designers to create complex structures with less material and energy than traditional manufacturing methods. Moreover, digital design tools and simulations can optimize product designs for efficiency and sustainability before physical prototypes are created, reducing waste in the development process.

Education and awareness are essential components of promoting sustainable design practices. By educating designers, manufacturers, and consumers about the benefits and importance of designing for minimal waste, the industry can shift towards more sustainable practices. Workshops, conferences, and online resources can provide valuable knowledge and inspiration for those looking to integrate sustainability into their work. Encouraging a culture of continuous learning and improvement is crucial for advancing sustainable design.

Government policies and regulations can also play a significant role in promoting sustainable design. By incentivizing the use of sustainable materials, supporting research and development, and enforcing waste reduction standards, governments can encourage manufacturers to adopt environmentally friendly practices. Collaboration between policymakers, industry leaders, and consumers is essential for creating a regulatory framework that supports sustainable design and drives meaningful change.

The journey towards designing products for minimal waste is a collaborative and ongoing effort that requires commitment from all stakeholders. By prioritizing sustainability in design, manufacturers can contribute to a more sustainable future, where resources are conserved, waste is minimized, and products are valued for their longevity and functionality. This shift not only benefits the environment but also aligns with consumer preferences, driving innovation and competitiveness in the market.

Embracing the principles of minimal waste design is not just a trend; it is a necessity for a sustainable future. As we continue to face environmental challenges, the need for innovative and responsible design becomes increasingly urgent. By reimagining the way products are designed, manufactured, and consumed, we can create a more sustainable world where waste is not an inevitable byproduct but a resource to be harnessed and valued.

Reducing Packaging Waste

Packaging waste is a significant contributor to environmental degradation, and addressing it is crucial for achieving sustainability goals. With the rise of consumerism and e-commerce, the volume of packaging waste has increased dramatically, making it imperative to adopt strategies that mitigate its impact. By focusing on reducing packaging waste, individuals and businesses can play a vital role in protecting the environment and conserving resources.

One of the most effective ways to reduce packaging waste is to eliminate unnecessary packaging altogether. This involves re-evaluating the need for packaging in various products and opting for minimalist designs that use fewer materials. For instance, some companies have successfully reduced packaging waste by using simple, unadorned wrappers for their products, demonstrating that less can often be more. By prioritizing functionality and simplicity, businesses can reduce the environmental footprint of their packaging.

Opting for reusable packaging is another powerful strategy. Reusable packaging systems, such as glass jars or metal tins, provide long-term solutions that can significantly cut down on waste. Once the product is consumed, the packaging can be returned, refilled, or repurposed, extending its lifecycle and reducing the demand for single-use materials. This approach has seen success in industries ranging from food and beverage to personal care, where consumers are increasingly seeking sustainable alternatives.

The selection of materials plays a crucial role in reducing packaging waste. Biodegradable and compostable materials offer environmentally friendly options that break down naturally, reducing the burden on landfills. Materials such as cornstarch, bamboo, and recycled paper are gaining popularity as they decompose without leaving harmful residues. By choosing these sustainable materials, businesses can align their practices with consumer values and environmental responsibilities.

Encouraging bulk purchasing is another effective method to minimize packaging waste. By offering products in larger quantities, businesses can reduce the ratio of packaging to product, resulting in less waste per unit consumed. Bulk purchasing is particularly effective for non-perishable goods, such as grains, nuts, and cleaning supplies. By providing consumers with the option to buy in bulk, retailers can decrease the overall packaging required while offering cost savings.

Innovative packaging designs that maximize efficiency and minimize waste are increasingly being adopted by forward-thinking companies. For example, collapsible or stackable packaging solutions reduce the volume of materials needed for transportation and storage. This not only cuts down on waste but also lowers transportation costs and carbon emissions. Additionally, smart packaging that communicates information through design rather than additional labels can reduce the need for excess materials.

Consumer education and engagement are vital components in the effort to reduce packaging waste. By raising awareness about the environmental impact of packaging and promoting responsible disposal practices, consumers can be empowered to make informed choices. Clear labeling and instructions on how to recycle or compost packaging can guide consumers towards sustainable disposal methods. Furthermore, sharing the environmental benefits of reduced packaging can motivate consumers to prioritize products with minimal packaging.

Businesses can take a proactive approach by assessing their current packaging practices and identifying areas for improvement. Conducting a packaging audit can reveal opportunities to reduce waste, whether through material substitutions, design modifications, or supply chain optimizations. Engaging with suppliers and stakeholders to explore sustainable alternatives can lead to innovative solutions that benefit both the environment and the bottom line.

Collaboration across industries and sectors is essential to drive systemic change in packaging waste reduction. Partnerships between manufacturers, retailers, policymakers, and consumers can foster the development of industry standards and best practices. By working together, stakeholders can create a unified approach to reducing packaging waste, sharing knowledge and resources to achieve common goals.

Regulations and policies also play a significant role in shaping packaging practices. Governments can incentivize waste reduction through tax breaks, grants, or recognition programs for businesses that adopt sustainable packaging solutions. Implementing extended producer responsibility (EPR) policies, where manufacturers are accountable for the disposal of their packaging, can encourage companies to design with the end-of-life in mind. These regulatory frameworks can drive innovation and accountability within the industry.

Ultimately, reducing packaging waste requires a shift in mindset from both producers and consumers. It involves recognizing that every piece of packaging has an environmental cost and that small changes can lead to significant impacts. By embracing sustainable practices and prioritizing waste reduction, we can create a future where packaging serves its purpose without burdening the planet. This transition not only benefits the environment but also aligns with the growing consumer demand for sustainable products and practices, paving the way for a more sustainable and responsible world.

Consumer Choices and Their Impact

Every purchase a consumer makes carries a ripple effect that extends far beyond the initial transaction. Consumer choices significantly impact the environment, economy, and society, shaping the world we live in. By making informed and conscious decisions, individuals can drive positive change and contribute to a more sustainable and equitable future.

The journey of a product begins long before it reaches the store shelves, encompassing the extraction of raw materials, manufacturing processes, transportation, and eventual disposal. Each of these stages carries its environmental toll. For instance, the production of electronics often involves the mining of rare minerals, which can lead to habitat destruction and pollution. Similarly, the fashion industry is notorious for its water-intensive processes and chemical use, affecting ecosystems and human health. By understanding the lifecycle of products, consumers can make choices that reduce their environmental impact.

One of the most direct ways to influence sustainability is through the selection of products made from eco-friendly materials. Opting for goods crafted from recycled, biodegradable, or sustainably sourced materials helps conserve resources and minimize waste. Whether it's choosing a bamboo toothbrush over a plastic one or selecting clothing made from organic cotton, these decisions collectively impact demand, encouraging manufacturers to adopt sustainable practices.

The importance of supporting ethical and sustainable brands cannot be overstated. Many companies are taking responsibility for their environmental and social impact, implementing fair labor practices, reducing waste, and minimizing their carbon footprint. By prioritizing purchases from these brands, consumers can support businesses that align with their values, sending a clear message that sustainability and ethics are crucial. This consumer demand can drive more companies to adopt responsible practices, fostering a marketplace that prioritizes people and the planet.

In addition to selecting sustainable products, reducing consumption is a powerful way to lessen one's environmental footprint. The minimalist movement encourages individuals to evaluate their needs and prioritize quality over quantity. By purchasing fewer, longer-lasting items, consumers can reduce waste and conserve resources. This mindset challenges the culture of disposability and promotes a more thoughtful approach to consumption, where each purchase is deliberate and meaningful.

Packaging is another critical factor in consumer choices. Opting for products with minimal or recyclable packaging can significantly reduce waste. Many companies are innovating with eco-friendly packaging solutions, such as compostable materials or reusable containers. Consumers can further support these efforts by choosing products packaged in materials that are easy to recycle or that offer refill options, contributing to the reduction of packaging waste.

The shift towards a circular economy presents exciting opportunities for consumers to engage in sustainable practices. By participating in product take-back programs, repair services, or second-hand markets, individuals can extend the lifecycle of products, reducing the need for new resources. This approach not only conserves materials but also supports a system where waste is viewed as a resource to be reused, recycled, or repurposed.

Food choices also play a significant role in environmental and social impact. The agricultural sector is a major contributor to greenhouse gas emissions, deforestation, and water usage. By choosing locally sourced, organic, and plant-based foods, consumers can reduce their carbon footprint and support sustainable farming practices. Additionally, reducing food waste through mindful meal planning and composting can further lessen the environmental impact of our diets.

Transportation choices are another area where consumers can make a difference. Opting for public transportation, carpooling, walking, or cycling can significantly reduce carbon emissions associated with personal vehicle use. For those who need to drive, choosing fuel-efficient or electric vehicles can contribute to cleaner air and reduced reliance on fossil fuels. These transportation decisions align with broader sustainability goals and demonstrate a commitment to reducing one's environmental impact.

Consumer advocacy and education are vital components in driving systemic change. By staying informed about the environmental and social implications of products and industries, consumers can make knowledgeable decisions that align with their values. Engaging in conversations, sharing information, and advocating for sustainable practices within communities can amplify the impact of individual choices. As awareness grows, the collective influence of consumers can lead to policy changes and industry shifts that prioritize sustainability.

The power of consumer choices lies in their ability to influence markets, drive innovation, and promote sustainable development. Each decision, whether it's the type of product purchased or the brand supported, contributes to shaping the world we inhabit. By embracing sustainable consumption habits, individuals can play an active role in creating a more equitable and environmentally responsible future. This journey towards conscious consumerism is one of empowerment and responsibility, where each choice is an opportunity to make a positive impact on the planet and the people who inhabit it.

Industrial Approaches to Waste Prevention

Industrial sectors play a critical role in waste prevention, as they are responsible for a significant portion of waste generated globally. By implementing effective waste prevention strategies, industries can reduce their environmental footprint, conserve resources, and even achieve cost savings. The key to success lies in adopting innovative approaches that integrate sustainability into every aspect of production and operations.

A cornerstone of industrial waste prevention is process optimization. By analyzing and refining production processes, industries can identify inefficiencies and areas where waste is generated. Lean manufacturing techniques, which focus on minimizing waste and maximizing productivity, are particularly effective in this regard. These techniques involve streamlining operations, reducing excess inventory, and improving workflow efficiency. As a result, industries can reduce waste output, lower costs, and improve overall productivity.

The adoption of cleaner production technologies is another crucial aspect of industrial waste prevention. These technologies aim to minimize waste and emissions by using resources more efficiently and reducing the generation of pollutants. For example, industries can implement closed-loop systems that recycle water and raw materials within the production process, reducing the need for fresh inputs and minimizing waste discharge. Additionally, investing in energy-efficient equipment and renewable energy sources can significantly reduce carbon emissions and enhance sustainability.

Material substitution is an innovative strategy that involves replacing hazardous or non-renewable materials with more sustainable alternatives. By selecting materials that are less harmful to the environment and human health, industries can reduce the environmental impact of their products. For instance, using biodegradable or recyclable materials in packaging and production processes can significantly decrease waste and pollution. This approach not only benefits the environment but also aligns with growing consumer demand for eco-friendly products.

Design for the environment (DfE) is a proactive approach that focuses on incorporating environmental considerations into product design. By designing products with their entire lifecycle in mind, industries can minimize waste generation from the outset. This includes selecting materials that are easy to recycle, designing products for disassembly, and reducing the use of toxic substances. By prioritizing sustainability in product design, industries can create products that are both environmentally friendly and economically viable.

Collaboration and partnerships are essential for driving industrial waste prevention. By working together, industries can share knowledge, resources, and best practices to achieve common sustainability goals. Collaborative initiatives, such as industrial symbiosis, involve the exchange of materials, energy, and by-products between different industries. This approach transforms waste from one industry into valuable inputs for another, creating a circular economy that reduces waste and conserves resources.

Employee engagement and training are vital components of successful waste prevention strategies. By fostering a culture of sustainability within the workplace, industries can empower employees to contribute to waste reduction efforts. Training programs that educate employees about waste prevention techniques, resource conservation, and environmental stewardship can enhance awareness and drive positive behavior change. Encouraging employee involvement in sustainability initiatives can lead to innovative solutions and a more sustainable organizational culture.

Policy and regulation play a significant role in shaping industrial waste prevention efforts. Governments can support industries by implementing policies that incentivize waste reduction and promote sustainable practices. These may include tax incentives for adopting cleaner technologies, grants for research and development, and regulations that set waste reduction targets. By creating a supportive policy environment, governments can encourage industries to invest in sustainability and drive systemic change.

The role of technology in industrial waste prevention cannot be overstated. Advances in digital technologies, such as the Internet of Things (IoT) and artificial intelligence, offer new opportunities for monitoring and optimizing resource use. IoT sensors can provide real-time data on energy consumption and waste generation, enabling industries to identify inefficiencies and make informed decisions. Similarly, predictive analytics can help industries anticipate waste generation and implement preventive measures, reducing waste before it occurs.

Life cycle assessment (LCA) is a valuable tool for evaluating the environmental impact of industrial processes and products. By assessing the entire lifecycle of a product, from raw material extraction to disposal, industries can identify areas for improvement and prioritize waste prevention efforts. LCA provides a comprehensive understanding of the environmental impact of production, enabling industries to make data-driven decisions that enhance sustainability.

Ultimately, industrial waste prevention requires a holistic approach that integrates sustainability into every aspect of operations. By adopting innovative practices, collaborating with stakeholders, and leveraging technology, industries can reduce waste, conserve resources, and contribute to a more sustainable future. This journey towards waste prevention is not only beneficial for the environment but also offers economic and social advantages, positioning industries as leaders in sustainability and responsible production.

Policies and Incentives for Source Reduction

Navigating the landscape of environmental sustainability, policies and incentives that focus on source reduction are pivotal in driving meaningful change across industries and communities. These mechanisms serve as catalysts, encouraging companies and individuals to adopt practices that minimize waste generation at the very beginning of the production and consumption process. By addressing the root cause of waste, source reduction initiatives offer a proactive approach to environmental conservation.

Governments play a crucial role in implementing policies that promote source reduction. Through legislation and regulatory frameworks, they can establish standards and guidelines that industries must adhere to. One effective strategy is the imposition of stringent waste reduction targets, compelling companies to reassess their production processes and identify opportunities for minimizing waste. These targets can be sector-specific, allowing for tailored approaches that consider the unique characteristics and challenges of different industries.

Financial incentives are powerful tools in encouraging source reduction. Tax breaks, subsidies, and grants can motivate businesses to invest in sustainable technologies and practices. For instance, companies that adopt energy-efficient manufacturing processes or sustainable materials can benefit from reduced tax liabilities or receive financial support for their efforts. These incentives lower the financial barriers associated with the transition to more sustainable practices, making it an attractive option for businesses.

Extended Producer Responsibility (EPR) is a policy approach that holds manufacturers accountable for the entire lifecycle of their products, including post-consumer waste. By requiring producers to manage the disposal and recycling of their products, EPR policies incentivize companies to design products with longevity, recyclability, and minimal waste in mind. This shift in responsibility encourages innovation and sustainable product design, ultimately leading to reduced waste generation.

Public awareness campaigns are instrumental in fostering a culture of source reduction. By educating consumers about the environmental impact of their choices and the benefits of reducing waste at the source, these campaigns can drive behavior change. Governments and non-governmental organizations (NGOs) can collaborate to develop educational materials, workshops, and events that promote sustainable consumption habits. An informed public is more likely to support and participate in initiatives that prioritize source reduction.

Collaboration between the public and private sectors is essential for the success of source reduction policies. Governments can work with industry leaders to develop voluntary agreements and partnerships that encourage sustainable practices. These collaborations can facilitate knowledge sharing, innovation, and the development of best practices that benefit both the environment and businesses. By aligning the interests of different stakeholders, these partnerships can create a unified approach to waste reduction.

Incentivizing research and development in sustainable technologies is another effective policy measure. By providing funding and support for innovation, governments can encourage the development of new materials, processes, and products that reduce waste generation. Research institutions and universities can play a significant role in advancing knowledge and technology in this area, contributing to the creation of a more sustainable future.

Standards and certifications can also drive source reduction by providing consumers and businesses with a clear understanding of what constitutes sustainable practices. Certifications such as ISO 14001 or ENERGY STAR can guide industries in implementing environmental management systems that prioritize waste reduction. These standards not only enhance transparency and accountability but also provide a competitive advantage to businesses that demonstrate their commitment to sustainability.

Local governments can implement community-level policies that promote source reduction. Initiatives such as pay-as-you-throw waste collection systems encourage residents to minimize waste by charging fees based on the amount of waste they generate. By incentivizing waste reduction at the household level, these programs can significantly decrease the volume of waste sent to landfills. Additionally, local governments can support community composting and recycling initiatives that contribute to waste reduction efforts.

The role of international cooperation in promoting source reduction cannot be overlooked. Global challenges require coordinated responses, and international agreements and frameworks can facilitate the exchange of knowledge, resources, and best practices. By working together, countries can develop harmonized policies and standards that address the environmental impact of waste on a global scale.

The journey towards effective source reduction is multifaceted, requiring a combination of policies, incentives, and collaborative efforts. By creating an enabling environment that supports sustainable practices, governments and stakeholders can drive systemic change that reduces waste generation and conserves resources. The impact of these efforts extends beyond environmental benefits, offering economic and social advantages that contribute to a more sustainable and equitable world. By embracing the principles of source reduction, we can pave the way for a future where waste is minimized, and resources are used wisely, ensuring a healthier planet for generations to come.

Chapter 3: Composting: Nature's Way of Recycling

Basics of Composting: What, Why, and How

Composting is an age-old practice that transforms organic waste into nutrient-rich soil, providing a natural way to recycle plant materials and reduce waste. Understanding the basics of composting is essential for anyone interested in sustainable living and gardening. The process not only diverts waste from landfills but also enriches the soil, supporting healthy plant growth and reducing the need for chemical fertilizers.

At its core, composting is the biological decomposition of organic matter by microorganisms, primarily bacteria and fungi, under controlled aerobic conditions. The resulting product, compost, is a dark, crumbly substance that resembles rich soil. It is an excellent soil amendment, improving soil structure, moisture retention, and nutrient content. Composting can be done on various scales, from small backyard bins to large industrial facilities, making it accessible to individuals and communities alike.

The materials suitable for composting are broadly categorized into two types: greens and browns. Greens are rich in nitrogen and include items like grass clippings, fruit and vegetable scraps, coffee grounds, and manure. Browns, on the other hand, provide carbon and consist of materials such as dried leaves, straw, wood chips, and paper. A balanced compost pile requires a mix of both, as nitrogen and carbon are essential for microbial activity and efficient decomposition.

To start composting, begin by selecting an appropriate location and container. For backyard composting, a shady, well-drained spot is ideal. Compost bins or piles can be constructed from wood, wire, or plastic, and should allow for adequate airflow and moisture retention. Some people choose to use tumblers, which are enclosed containers that can be rotated to mix the compost materials easily. Whichever method you choose, ensure the composting setup is convenient and suitable for your space.

Layering is crucial in building a compost pile. Begin with a layer of coarse browns, such as twigs or straw, to facilitate drainage and airflow. Follow with alternating layers of greens and browns, ensuring the pile remains moist but not waterlogged. A good rule of thumb is to aim for a ratio of about 3 parts browns to 1 part greens. Mixing the pile periodically with a garden fork or shovel aerates the compost, encouraging decomposition and preventing unpleasant odors.

Moisture is a key factor in successful composting. The pile should be kept as damp as a wrung-out sponge, as too little moisture will slow decomposition, while too much can lead to anaerobic conditions and odor problems. In dry climates or during periods of low rainfall, you may need to water the compost pile to maintain the appropriate moisture level. Conversely, in wet climates, covering the pile with a tarp can help prevent excessive moisture.

Temperature is another critical component of the composting process. As microorganisms break down the organic matter, they generate heat. A well-maintained compost pile can reach temperatures between 130°F and 160°F, which is ideal for killing pathogens and weed seeds. Regularly turning the pile helps maintain these temperatures by introducing oxygen and redistributing heat. Compost thermometers are available for those interested in monitoring the temperature of their pile closely.

The benefits of composting extend beyond waste reduction and soil improvement. Composting reduces methane emissions from landfills, a potent greenhouse gas contributing to climate change. By returning organic matter to the earth, composting also supports biodiversity, as healthy soil teems with beneficial microbes, insects, and fungi. Moreover, using compost in gardens and landscapes encourages healthier plants, which are more resistant to pests and diseases.

For those living in urban areas or without access to outdoor space, vermicomposting offers an alternative method. This process uses worms, typically red wigglers, to break down organic waste in a controlled, indoor environment. Vermicomposting bins are compact and can be placed under kitchen sinks or in basements, making it an accessible option for apartment dwellers. The resulting worm castings are highly nutrient-rich and can be used as a potent fertilizer for houseplants or small gardens.

Composting is not without its challenges. Common issues include foul odors, pests, and slow decomposition. These problems often arise from imbalances in the compost pile, such as excess moisture, insufficient aeration, or an improper ratio of greens to browns. Addressing these issues typically involves adjusting the composition of the pile, turning it more frequently, or adding dry materials to absorb excess moisture.

As more people become aware of the environmental impact of waste, composting is gaining popularity as a simple yet effective solution. Educational workshops, community composting programs, and online resources are available to help beginners get started and troubleshoot common issues. By adopting composting practices, individuals can contribute to a more sustainable world, one nutrient-rich pile at a time. The basics of composting are straightforward, and with a little patience and experimentation, anyone can transform their organic waste into a valuable resource that benefits both their garden and the environment.

Home Composting Techniques

Transforming kitchen scraps and yard waste into nutrient-rich compost is a rewarding endeavor that benefits both the environment and the home gardener. Home composting techniques offer a practical way to reduce waste, enrich soils, and cultivate a more sustainable lifestyle. Understanding the nuances of different composting methods allows individuals to tailor their approach to their specific living conditions and needs, making it accessible to everyone, regardless of space constraints.

Traditional backyard composting is one of the most common methods employed by homeowners. This technique involves creating a compost pile or using a bin in an outdoor space. The process begins with selecting an appropriate location— preferably a level, well-drained area that receives some shade. A simple bin can be made from repurposed materials like wooden pallets or purchased from garden centers. The key to successful composting is maintaining a balance between green and brown materials. Greens, which are nitrogen-rich, include items like vegetable scraps, coffee grounds, and grass clippings. Browns, which provide carbon, consist of dried leaves, straw, and cardboard. Layering these materials alternately ensures that the compost pile has the right mix for efficient decomposition.

To speed up the composting process, it's crucial to turn the pile regularly. This aerates the compost, providing oxygen to the microorganisms that break down the organic matter. A garden fork or shovel is often used for this purpose. Moisture levels should be monitored to keep the pile as damp as a wrung-out sponge. If the pile becomes too dry, a sprinkle of water can help maintain the necessary conditions for microbial activity. Conversely, if the pile is too wet, adding more browns can absorb excess moisture.

For those with limited outdoor space, container or bin composting offers a compact solution. These systems are ideal for small yards or urban environments where space is at a premium. Compost bins come in various sizes and designs, often featuring lids and ventilation holes to manage odors and ensure proper airflow. The same principles of layering greens and browns apply, and regular mixing helps maintain the balance. Container composting is relatively low-maintenance and can produce compost within a few months, depending on factors like temperature and material composition.

Vermicomposting is another excellent option for individuals living in apartments or those without access to outdoor space. This method uses worms, typically red wigglers, to break down organic waste in a controlled indoor environment. A vermicomposting bin can be kept indoors, allowing for year-round composting. These bins are compact and require minimal space, making them suitable for kitchens, balconies, or basements. Worms consume organic matter and produce castings, which are a highly nutritious form of compost. To start, individuals need a bin, bedding material like shredded newspaper or coconut coir, and a population of worms. Regular feeding with kitchen scraps and periodic maintenance, such as adding fresh bedding and harvesting castings, keeps the system thriving.

For those with more ambitious composting goals, hot composting is an accelerated method that produces compost in a matter of weeks rather than months. This technique requires a larger volume of material and more diligent management. The compost pile needs to reach temperatures between 130°F and 160°F to effectively break down organic matter and kill pathogens and weed seeds. Achieving these temperatures involves creating a large pile, at least three cubic feet in size, and maintaining an optimal balance of greens and browns. Frequent turning, every few days, is necessary to sustain the high temperatures and speed up decomposition. While hot composting demands more effort, the rapid production of finished compost makes it an attractive option for avid gardeners.

Trench composting offers a less conventional approach, ideal for those who prefer a low-maintenance method. In this technique, organic waste is buried directly in the soil, allowing it to decompose naturally underground. Trench composting can be done in vegetable gardens or flower beds, enriching the soil in situ. Digging a trench or hole, filling it with organic waste, and covering it with soil is all that's needed. This method is particularly useful for disposing of kitchen scraps without attracting pests or requiring a dedicated compost bin.

For communities or neighborhoods looking to collaborate, communal composting offers a way to pool resources and share the benefits of composting. Community gardens or shared spaces can host larger composting systems that accommodate waste from multiple households. This approach fosters community engagement and sustainability education, as participants contribute to and benefit from the collective effort. Communal composting systems can vary in size and complexity, from simple piles to more elaborate setups with dedicated bins and turning mechanisms.

Regardless of the method chosen, troubleshooting is an integral part of successful composting. Common challenges include foul odors, pests, and slow decomposition. Odors typically arise from an imbalance in the compost pile, often due to excess moisture or lack of aeration. Adjusting the mix of materials or turning the pile can alleviate this issue. Pests, such as rodents or insects, can be deterred by avoiding meat and dairy scraps and ensuring that food waste is adequately covered with browns. If decomposition is slow, adding more greens or turning the pile can stimulate microbial activity.

Home composting techniques not only reduce household waste but also contribute to healthier gardens and landscapes. The resulting compost enhances soil fertility, structure, and moisture retention, leading to more robust plant growth and reduced reliance on chemical fertilizers. By embracing composting, individuals can transform waste into a valuable resource, fostering a more sustainable and environmentally conscious lifestyle. The art of composting, with its diverse methods and benefits, offers a tangible way to make a positive impact on the planet, one handful of rich, dark soil at a time.

Community and Urban Composting Programs

In the face of mounting environmental challenges and urbanization, community and urban composting programs have emerged as innovative solutions to manage organic waste effectively. These programs not only reduce the burden on landfills but also foster a sense of community involvement and environmental stewardship. By turning waste into a resource, urban composting initiatives contribute to sustainable city living and provide an avenue for residents to engage actively in environmental conservation.

Urban composting programs are often initiated by municipalities, non-profit organizations, or local community groups. They aim to provide residents with the tools and knowledge needed to compost in densely populated areas where space is limited. These programs can take many forms, from neighborhood composting hubs to city-wide collection services that gather organic waste from households and businesses.

The success of community composting programs hinges on effective education and outreach. Residents must be informed about the benefits of composting and how they can participate. Workshops, demonstrations, and informational materials can play a significant role in raising awareness and encouraging participation. By demystifying the composting process and highlighting its positive impact on the environment, organizers can inspire community members to get involved.

One of the primary challenges in urban composting is space constraints. Limited outdoor areas and a lack of private gardens make traditional backyard composting unfeasible for many city dwellers. To address this, community composting programs often establish centralized composting sites where residents can drop off their organic waste. These sites serve as communal resources, managed by volunteers or program staff, and are equipped with compost bins or tumblers to handle large volumes of waste.

Urban composting programs also benefit significantly from partnerships with local governments and waste management services. By collaborating with city officials, programs can integrate composting into existing waste collection systems, making it easier for residents to participate. Some cities offer curbside collection of organic waste, where residents place their compostable materials in designated bins for pickup. This approach streamlines the composting process and increases participation by removing logistical barriers.

Innovative solutions, such as rooftop gardens and vertical composting systems, offer creative ways to incorporate composting into urban environments. Rooftop gardens can utilize compost produced from organic waste to enrich the soil, creating a closed-loop system that benefits both the building and the environment. Similarly, vertical composting systems, which stack compost bins to maximize space efficiency, are ideal for urban areas with limited ground space.

Community gardens are another vital component of urban composting programs. These shared spaces provide a practical application for compost, enhancing soil fertility and supporting local food production. Community gardens often serve as focal points for composting initiatives, where participants can learn about sustainable agriculture practices and witness the tangible benefits of their composting efforts. By integrating composting with urban agriculture, these programs promote food security and resilience within the community.

Technology and digital platforms can enhance the effectiveness of urban composting programs by facilitating communication and coordination. Mobile apps and online portals can connect residents with composting resources, track participation, and provide feedback on waste reduction efforts. These tools can also be used to organize events, schedule drop-offs, and share best practices among community members, fostering a sense of collaboration and shared responsibility.

Inclusivity and accessibility are crucial factors in designing successful community composting programs. Efforts should be made to ensure that all residents, regardless of socioeconomic status or physical ability, can participate. Offering resources in multiple languages, providing accessible drop-off points, and supporting low-income neighborhoods with composting supplies can help bridge gaps and promote widespread engagement. Inclusivity not only broadens participation but also strengthens community bonds and promotes social equity.

Measuring the impact of urban composting programs is essential for assessing their success and identifying areas for improvement. Metrics such as the volume of waste diverted from landfills, the amount of compost produced, and the number of participants can provide valuable insights into the program's effectiveness. Regular evaluation allows organizers to refine their strategies, celebrate achievements, and communicate the program's benefits to stakeholders and potential supporters.

Community and urban composting programs offer a compelling model for sustainable waste management in cities. By harnessing the collective power of residents, these initiatives transform organic waste into a valuable resource, reducing environmental impact and enhancing urban ecosystems. The collaborative nature of community composting fosters a sense of shared responsibility and empowerment, encouraging individuals to take an active role in creating a more sustainable future. As cities continue to grow and face the challenges of waste management, urban composting programs represent a practical and scalable solution that benefits both people and the planet.

Composting in Schools and Institutions

Integrating composting into schools and institutions is a dynamic way to teach sustainability, reduce waste, and promote environmental stewardship among students and staff. By establishing composting programs in educational and institutional settings, we can inspire a new generation to embrace eco-friendly practices, while simultaneously addressing the practical issue of waste management. These programs offer hands-on learning opportunities that align with curricula across various subjects, making them an invaluable educational tool.

The first step in implementing a composting program in schools and institutions is gaining the support of key stakeholders. This includes administrators, teachers, staff, students, and even parents. Presenting the benefits of composting—such as reducing waste, saving money on waste disposal, and enhancing educational experiences—can help garner enthusiasm and buy-in. Schools can also highlight how composting aligns with their sustainability goals and mission statements, reinforcing the institution's commitment to environmental responsibility.

Once support is established, identifying a suitable location for composting is crucial. Schools with outdoor spaces can consider traditional composting bins or piles, which can be managed by students and staff. For those with limited space, vermicomposting offers a compact and efficient solution. Worm bins can be placed indoors, providing a year-round composting option that is easy to maintain. These systems are particularly well-suited for classrooms, as they allow students to observe the composting process up close.

Incorporating composting into the curriculum enhances student learning and engagement. Science classes can explore the biology of decomposition, examining the role of microorganisms and the conditions necessary for effective composting. Math lessons can incorporate data collection and analysis, allowing students to track the volume of waste diverted or measure temperature changes in the compost pile. Language arts classes can engage students in writing assignments about their composting experiences or the broader environmental impact of waste reduction.

Hands-on involvement is key to the success of composting programs in schools and institutions. Students can be tasked with collecting food scraps from cafeterias, managing compost bins, and monitoring the decomposition process. This experiential learning fosters a sense of ownership and responsibility, as students see firsthand the positive impact of their efforts. Gardening clubs or environmental groups can take on leadership roles, organizing activities and educating their peers about the importance of composting.

To ensure the program runs smoothly, establishing clear guidelines and responsibilities is essential. A designated coordinator, such as a teacher or staff member, can oversee the program and facilitate communication among participants. Developing a schedule for tasks like waste collection, bin maintenance, and compost monitoring helps ensure that responsibilities are shared and that the program remains sustainable over time. Training sessions or workshops can equip students and staff with the knowledge and skills needed to manage the composting process effectively.

Community partnerships can enhance composting programs in schools and institutions by providing additional resources and support. Local waste management agencies, environmental organizations, or businesses may offer expertise, funding, or supplies like compost bins and educational materials. These partnerships can also create opportunities for field trips, guest speakers, or collaborative projects that enrich the educational experience and strengthen community ties.

Evaluating the program's impact is important for demonstrating its value and identifying areas for improvement. Metrics such as the amount of waste diverted from landfills, the quantity of compost produced, and the level of student engagement can provide insights into the program's success. Sharing these results with the school community and stakeholders reinforces the benefits of composting and encourages continued participation.

Composting programs also offer institutions the chance to model sustainable practices, setting an example for students and the wider community. By incorporating composting into daily operations, schools can demonstrate the feasibility and benefits of waste reduction strategies, inspiring others to take action. This leadership role not only enhances the institution's reputation but also contributes to a broader cultural shift towards sustainability.

The environmental and educational benefits of composting in schools and institutions are manifold. By reducing waste, enriching the soil, and fostering ecological awareness, these programs contribute to a more sustainable future. Moreover, they empower students with the knowledge and skills to make environmentally conscious decisions, nurturing a generation of informed and responsible citizens. As composting becomes an integral part of school and institutional life, it lays the groundwork for lasting change, transforming waste into a valuable resource and cultivating a culture of sustainability.

Benefits of Composting for Soil and Environment

Composting stands as a beacon of sustainability, transforming organic waste into a valuable resource that rejuvenates the soil and mitigates environmental challenges. The benefits of composting extend beyond waste reduction, touching various aspects of ecological health and resource management. Understanding these advantages not only encourages more widespread adoption of composting practices but also highlights the profound impact they can have on our planet.

At the heart of composting's benefits lies its ability to enrich soil. Compost, often referred to as "black gold," is a nutrient-rich amendment that improves soil structure, fertility, and biodiversity. When added to soil, compost enhances its texture, making it more porous and better able to retain moisture. This improved structure reduces soil compaction, promotes root growth, and enhances the soil's ability to hold water, which is particularly beneficial in arid regions or during periods of drought. As a result, plants grown in compost-amended soil typically exhibit stronger growth, increased resilience to pests and diseases, and higher yields.

Beyond physical improvements, compost also contributes a wealth of nutrients essential for plant health. It serves as a slow-release fertilizer, providing a steady supply of nitrogen, phosphorus, potassium, and micronutrients. Unlike synthetic fertilizers, compost releases nutrients at a rate that aligns with plant needs, reducing the risk of nutrient leaching and waterway pollution. This natural balance supports sustainable agriculture by minimizing dependency on chemical inputs and fostering healthier ecosystems.

The presence of organic matter in compost is a boon for soil biodiversity. Compost introduces a diverse array of beneficial microorganisms, fungi, and insects into the soil ecosystem. These organisms play crucial roles in breaking down organic matter, cycling nutrients, and maintaining soil health. By enhancing microbial activity, compost fosters a living soil environment that supports plant growth and resilience. This biodiversity also aids in suppressing soil-borne diseases, as a healthy microbial community can outcompete and inhibit pathogenic organisms.

Composting also plays a vital role in reducing greenhouse gas emissions and combating climate change. Organic waste in landfills decomposes anaerobically, producing methane, a potent greenhouse gas. By diverting organic waste from landfills through composting, we significantly reduce methane emissions. Furthermore, composting sequesters carbon in the soil, helping to offset carbon dioxide emissions. This dual benefit underscores composting as a practical climate action strategy that contributes to global efforts to reduce greenhouse gas emissions.

Erosion control is another significant environmental benefit of composting. The improved soil structure and increased organic matter content resulting from compost application enhance soil stability and reduce erosion. This is particularly important in areas prone to wind or water erosion, where soil loss can lead to decreased agricultural productivity and degraded landscapes. By preventing erosion, composting helps maintain soil fertility and protect water quality by reducing sediment runoff into waterways.

Composting also contributes to waste reduction and resource conservation. By transforming organic waste into compost, we reduce the volume of waste sent to landfills and incinerators, conserving valuable landfill space and reducing disposal costs. This reduction in waste also lowers the environmental impact of waste management processes, including transportation and energy use. By recycling organic materials, composting closes the nutrient loop, returning valuable resources to the soil and reducing the need for virgin materials in agriculture and landscaping.

In urban environments, composting offers unique benefits by supporting green infrastructure and sustainable city living. Compost can be used in urban gardens, rooftop farms, and green spaces, enhancing soil quality and supporting plant growth in areas with poor or contaminated soils. These green spaces provide numerous ecosystem services, including air and water purification, temperature regulation, and habitat for urban wildlife. By integrating composting into urban planning, cities can create more resilient and sustainable environments that improve the quality of life for their residents.

The educational and community-building aspects of composting should not be overlooked. Composting programs in schools, community gardens, and neighborhoods foster environmental awareness and stewardship. They provide hands-on learning opportunities that teach participants about ecological processes, resource management, and sustainable practices. By engaging communities in composting, we cultivate a culture of sustainability and collective responsibility, empowering individuals to take action and make a positive impact on their environment.

Ultimately, the benefits of composting for soil and the environment are profound and multifaceted. From enhancing soil health and fertility to reducing greenhouse gas emissions and waste, composting offers a powerful tool for addressing environmental challenges. By embracing composting practices, we not only improve the health of our soils and ecosystems but also contribute to a more sustainable and resilient future for our planet. The journey from waste to resource is one of transformation and renewal, embodying the principles of sustainability and the promise of a healthier, more balanced world.

Chapter 4: Waste Audits and Analysis

Conducting a Waste Audit: Step-by-Step Guide

Conducting a waste audit is a pivotal step in understanding the composition and volume of waste produced by a household, school, business, or community. By systematically examining waste, we can identify opportunities for waste reduction, recycling, and composting, ultimately leading to more sustainable waste management practices. This chapter offers a comprehensive guide to conducting a waste audit, providing practical advice and actionable steps for beginners to embark on this enlightening journey.

A successful waste audit begins with setting clear objectives. Determine the scope of the audit by deciding which areas or departments will be assessed. Establish specific goals, such as reducing overall waste, increasing recycling rates, or identifying materials suitable for composting. Engaging stakeholders—whether they are family members, colleagues, or community participants—in the planning process fosters collaboration and ensures that the audit aligns with shared sustainability objectives.

Once the objectives are set, gather the necessary materials and assemble a team to conduct the audit. Essential items include gloves, tarps or plastic sheets, data collection forms, and scales for weighing waste. Depending on the size of the audit, team members may be assigned specific roles, such as sorting, recording data, or managing logistics. A diverse team encourages different perspectives and insights, enriching the audit process.

Choose a suitable location and time for the audit, ensuring that it is safe and convenient for all participants. The area should be spacious enough to accommodate waste sorting and should provide adequate ventilation. Consider conducting the audit after a typical day or week of waste generation to capture a representative sample. This timing ensures that the data collected reflects the regular waste habits of the environment being audited.

Begin the audit by collecting waste from the designated areas. Gather waste from bins, receptacles, and collection points, and transport it to the audit location. If possible, sort waste indoors to minimize disruption and ensure safety from external elements. Categorize waste into specific streams, such as recyclables, compostables, landfill waste, and hazardous materials. This initial sorting allows for a detailed analysis of each waste category during the audit.

With waste sorted into categories, conduct a detailed examination of each stream. Analyze the contents to identify common items and patterns in waste generation. For instance, an audit may reveal significant quantities of paper waste, food scraps, or single-use plastics. Note the frequency and volume of these items, as well as any anomalies or unexpected findings. This analysis provides valuable insights into consumption habits and highlights areas for improvement.

Weigh each category of waste and record the data meticulously. Accurate measurements are critical for assessing the overall waste footprint and identifying potential reduction strategies. Use scales to obtain precise weights, and document the data systematically using forms or digital tools. This quantitative data complements qualitative observations, offering a comprehensive view of waste generation patterns.

After completing the audit, analyze the data to identify trends and opportunities for waste reduction. Consider both the short-term and long-term implications of the findings. For example, if a large proportion of waste is compostable, implementing a composting program could significantly reduce waste sent to landfills. Similarly, identifying high volumes of recyclable materials may indicate the need for improved recycling education or infrastructure.

Develop an action plan based on the audit's findings, prioritizing initiatives that align with the objectives set at the outset. Engage stakeholders in the decision-making process to ensure buy-in and commitment to the proposed strategies. The action plan should include specific goals, timelines, and responsibilities for implementing waste reduction measures. Regularly review and update the plan to reflect progress and adapt to changing circumstances.

Communicate the results of the waste audit to all relevant stakeholders. Share key findings, insights, and recommendations in a clear and accessible format. Use visual aids, such as charts or infographics, to convey data effectively. Transparent communication fosters awareness and accountability, motivating stakeholders to take action and support sustainability initiatives.

A waste audit is not a one-time event but an ongoing process of evaluation and improvement. Schedule regular audits to monitor progress and assess the effectiveness of waste reduction strategies. Use the insights gained from each audit to refine practices, celebrate achievements, and identify new opportunities for improvement.

Conducting a waste audit is a transformative experience that sheds light on the hidden realities of waste generation and disposal. By examining waste systematically, individuals and organizations gain a deeper understanding of their environmental impact and identify tangible ways to reduce it. The insights garnered from a waste audit empower participants to make informed decisions, fostering a culture of sustainability and resourcefulness.

Waste audits also serve as powerful educational tools, raising awareness about consumption patterns and the importance of waste reduction. By involving a broad range of participants in the process, audits cultivate a sense of shared responsibility and inspire collective action. As waste audits become more widespread, they contribute to a broader cultural shift towards sustainable living and environmental stewardship.

The journey of conducting a waste audit is one of discovery and empowerment. By taking the time to meticulously examine waste, we unlock the potential to transform our habits and create positive change. Each piece of waste tells a story, and by listening to these stories, we can chart a path towards a more sustainable and resilient future. The power to reduce waste and conserve resources lies in our hands, and a waste audit is the first step in harnessing that power for the greater good.

Data Collection and Analysis Techniques

Gathering and analyzing data is a foundational aspect of understanding and improving composting practices. Data collection and analysis techniques provide insights into the efficiency and impact of composting systems, enabling informed decisions and fostering continual improvement. By employing robust methodologies, individuals and organizations can optimize their composting efforts, reduce waste, and contribute to environmental sustainability.

The process of data collection begins with defining clear objectives and identifying the specific metrics that will be measured. These metrics might include the volume and type of organic waste collected, the rate of decomposition, temperature fluctuations within the compost pile, and the quality of the finished compost. By establishing clear goals, such as reducing waste output or improving compost quality, the data collection process becomes more focused and meaningful.

Selecting appropriate tools and methods for data collection is crucial. For measuring waste volume, scales and measuring containers can provide precise data. Compost thermometers are essential for monitoring temperature, an important indicator of microbial activity and decomposition efficiency. Regular temperature readings help determine whether the composting process is proceeding optimally or if adjustments are needed. Additionally, moisture meters can be used to assess water content, ensuring that the compost remains within the ideal range for aerobic decomposition.

Recording data consistently and accurately is vital for meaningful analysis. Establishing a routine for data collection, such as daily or weekly checks, helps maintain consistency and reliability. Data should be documented in a systematic manner, whether through spreadsheets, notebooks, or digital applications. This organized approach not only facilitates analysis but also allows for easy reference and comparison over time.

Once data is collected, the analysis phase begins. Analyzing waste volume data can reveal patterns and trends in waste generation, highlighting opportunities for reduction or diversion. For example, identifying peak waste production times might indicate a need for targeted waste reduction initiatives during those periods. Analyzing temperature data can help determine the efficiency of the composting process and identify any issues that require intervention, such as insufficient aeration or moisture imbalance.

Visualizing data through charts and graphs enhances understanding and communication. Graphical representations make it easier to identify trends, patterns, and anomalies in the data. For instance, a temperature graph over time can illustrate the stages of the composting process, helping to pinpoint when the pile reaches peak decomposition and when it stabilizes. Visualizations can also be used to communicate findings to stakeholders, facilitating discussions about improvements and adjustments.

Advanced data analysis techniques, such as statistical analysis, can provide deeper insights into composting systems. Statistical tools can be employed to assess correlations between variables, such as the relationship between moisture levels and decomposition rates. This analysis can inform decisions about optimal conditions for composting, leading to more efficient and effective processes. Additionally, statistical analysis can help evaluate the impact of changes or interventions, providing evidence-based recommendations for improvement.

For those conducting data analysis in larger-scale operations, software tools and technologies can streamline processes and enhance accuracy. Data management software can automate data collection, storage, and analysis, reducing the potential for human error and increasing efficiency. These tools often include features for tracking and reporting, which can simplify the process of monitoring progress and communicating results.

Feedback loops are an integral part of the data collection and analysis process. By using data to inform decisions and then monitoring the outcomes, composting systems can undergo continuous improvement. This iterative approach allows for experimentation and adaptation, fostering resilience and innovation. For example, if temperature data indicates that the compost pile is not heating adequately, adjustments can be made to the carbon-to-nitrogen ratio or aeration practices, and subsequent data collection can assess the impact of these changes.

Engaging stakeholders in the data collection and analysis process can enhance buy-in and collaboration. By involving team members, community participants, or organizational leaders in data discussions, diverse perspectives and insights can be incorporated into decision-making. This collaborative approach not only enriches the analysis but also fosters a shared commitment to achieving sustainability goals.

Data collection and analysis techniques play a crucial role in optimizing composting practices and achieving sustainability objectives. By systematically gathering and interpreting data, individuals and organizations can enhance the efficiency and effectiveness of their composting efforts, reduce waste, and contribute to a healthier environment. The insights gained from data analysis empower stakeholders to make informed decisions, fostering a culture of continuous improvement and innovation in composting systems. As data-driven practices become more widespread, they hold the potential to transform composting into a more precise and impactful tool for sustainability.

Identifying Key Areas for Waste Reduction

Embarking on the journey of waste reduction begins with identifying key areas where waste is generated. This proactive approach not only minimizes environmental impact but also fosters efficient resource use and cost savings. Understanding the sources and types of waste produced in homes, businesses, and communities allows for targeted strategies that yield significant reductions. By focusing on these pivotal areas, individuals and organizations can make meaningful strides toward sustainability.

In residential settings, the kitchen emerges as a primary area for waste generation. Food waste constitutes a substantial portion of household waste, often resulting from over-purchasing, improper storage, or simply forgetting leftovers. Conducting an inventory of kitchen habits can illuminate opportunities for waste reduction. Implementing meal planning and shopping lists can prevent impulsive buying, while proper storage techniques extend the shelf life of perishable items. Additionally, utilizing leftovers creatively reduces waste and maximizes the value of groceries.

Packaging waste is another significant contributor to household waste. Modern lifestyles have led to an increase in single-use packaging, particularly from takeout meals and convenience foods. Identifying and addressing this area involves reconsidering purchasing habits and opting for products with minimal or recyclable packaging. Bulk buying and refilling containers can drastically reduce packaging waste, while choosing reusable alternatives—such as cloth bags, glass jars, and beeswax wraps—can further mitigate the impact.

The home office and study area also produce waste, primarily in the form of paper and electronic waste. Transitioning to digital documentation and communication reduces paper consumption, while responsibly recycling or donating old electronics prevents them from ending up in landfills. Encouragingly, many communities offer e-waste recycling programs, making it easier to dispose of electronics in an environmentally friendly manner. Implementing a "think before you print" policy can significantly cut down on unnecessary paper usage.

In business and commercial environments, waste reduction efforts often focus on operational practices and supply chains. Offices can reduce paper waste by digitizing processes, promoting double-sided printing, and implementing document management systems that streamline digital storage. In manufacturing and production settings, assessing supply chains for inefficiencies and wasteful practices can lead to significant reductions. This might involve working with suppliers to reduce packaging, optimizing transportation routes, or employing lean manufacturing principles to minimize excess production.

Restaurants and food service establishments face unique waste challenges, particularly with food and packaging waste.

Conducting waste audits can help identify common sources of waste, such as spoiled inventory or surplus food. Implementing portion control, donating excess food to local charities, and adopting composting practices can greatly reduce waste. Additionally, transitioning to reusable or compostable packaging and utensils can lessen the environmental impact of takeout and delivery services.

Schools and educational institutions have the opportunity to instill waste reduction habits in students while reducing institutional waste. Initiatives such as recycling programs, composting, and waste-free lunch days can engage students and staff in sustainability efforts. Educators can incorporate waste reduction into the curriculum, teaching students about the lifecycle of products and the importance of resource conservation. These efforts not only reduce waste but also cultivate a culture of environmental stewardship among future generations.

Communities can address waste at a larger scale by promoting waste reduction initiatives and infrastructure. Establishing community composting sites, recycling centers, and swap meets encourages residents to participate actively in waste reduction efforts. Public awareness campaigns and workshops can educate residents about the impact of waste and the benefits of reduction strategies. Engaging local businesses and organizations in community-wide initiatives fosters collaboration and amplifies the impact of individual efforts.

The role of technology in waste reduction cannot be overlooked. Apps and digital platforms can facilitate waste tracking and management, providing users with insights into their consumption patterns and areas for improvement. Smart bins and sensors can monitor waste levels in real-time, optimizing collection routes and reducing unnecessary pickups. Technology also enables the sharing economy, allowing individuals to exchange or rent items rather than purchasing new ones, thereby reducing waste generation.

An essential aspect of identifying key areas for waste reduction is setting measurable goals and tracking progress. Establishing clear targets—such as reducing household waste by a certain percentage or achieving zero waste in specific departments—provides motivation and direction. Regularly evaluating progress through audits or data analysis ensures accountability and allows for adjustments to strategies as needed. Celebrating milestones and achievements reinforces commitment and encourages continued efforts.

Ultimately, waste reduction is a collaborative endeavor that requires the involvement of individuals, businesses, and communities. By identifying key areas of waste generation and implementing targeted strategies, we can make significant progress toward a more sustainable future. The journey requires creativity, commitment, and adaptability, but the rewards—reduced environmental impact, cost savings, and a healthier planet—are well worth the effort. As we become more attuned to the sources and impacts of waste, we empower ourselves to take meaningful action and inspire others to join the movement.

Setting Targets and Measuring Progress

Setting targets and measuring progress are essential components of any successful waste reduction initiative. They provide a structured framework for identifying objectives, tracking improvements, and maintaining accountability. By establishing clear goals and implementing effective measurement techniques, individuals and organizations can drive meaningful change, fostering a culture of sustainability and continuous improvement.

The first step in setting waste reduction targets is to conduct a thorough assessment of the current situation. This involves analyzing past and current waste generation data to identify baseline levels and patterns. Through waste audits or data collection exercises, you can gain insights into the types and volumes of waste produced, pinpointing areas with the greatest potential for reduction. This foundational knowledge is crucial for setting realistic and achievable targets tailored to specific circumstances.

Once the baseline is established, it's time to define specific, measurable, achievable, relevant, and time-bound (SMART) targets. These targets should reflect both short-term and long-term goals, providing a roadmap for incremental progress. For example, a household might aim to reduce kitchen waste by 25% within six months by implementing meal planning and composting. Meanwhile, a business might target a 50% reduction in paper use over a year by transitioning to digital processes.

It's important to involve all stakeholders in the target-setting process. Engaging team members, community participants, or organizational leaders fosters a sense of ownership and commitment to the goals. Collaborative dialogue encourages diverse perspectives and creative solutions, ensuring that targets are comprehensive and aligned with the values and capabilities of the group. This collective approach not only enhances buy-in but also promotes a shared sense of purpose and motivation.

Once targets are set, developing a strategy to achieve them is essential. This strategy should outline the specific actions, resources, and timelines required to meet the objectives. It should also account for potential challenges and contingencies, allowing for flexibility and adaptation as circumstances change. By breaking down the goals into actionable steps, the strategy becomes a practical guide for implementation, empowering stakeholders to take concrete action.

Measuring progress is key to ensuring that targets are met and that the waste reduction initiative remains on track. Regular monitoring and data collection provide valuable feedback on the effectiveness of the strategies implemented. This ongoing assessment allows for timely adjustments and interventions, optimizing the impact of the initiative. For instance, if data indicates that waste reduction is not progressing as expected, it may be necessary to revise tactics or provide additional resources or support.

Tracking tools and technologies can enhance the measurement process, providing accurate and efficient data collection and analysis. Digital platforms, spreadsheets, or specialized software can streamline the recording and reporting of waste data, enabling easy visualization and comparison over time. These tools facilitate transparency and accountability, ensuring that stakeholders remain informed and engaged in the progress of the initiative.

Regularly reviewing and analyzing the data collected is crucial for understanding trends, successes, and areas for improvement. This analysis provides insights into the factors driving progress or hindering achievement, informing decisions about future actions. By identifying patterns and correlations, stakeholders can refine strategies and focus efforts on the most impactful interventions. Celebrating milestones and successes along the way reinforces motivation and commitment, recognizing the hard work and dedication of all involved.

Communication plays a vital role in maintaining momentum and engagement throughout the waste reduction initiative. Sharing progress updates, challenges, and achievements with stakeholders fosters a sense of community and shared responsibility. Transparent communication builds trust and encourages collaboration, creating a supportive environment for continuous improvement. Whether through meetings, newsletters, or social media, effective communication keeps everyone informed and invested in the success of the initiative.

As targets are met, it's important to reassess and set new goals to maintain progress and drive further improvements. Waste reduction is an ongoing journey, and continuous evaluation ensures that efforts remain relevant and impactful. By regularly revisiting and updating targets, individuals and organizations can adapt to changing circumstances and priorities, sustaining momentum and commitment to sustainability.

Ultimately, setting targets and measuring progress are dynamic processes that empower individuals and organizations to achieve their waste reduction goals. By establishing clear objectives, implementing effective measurement techniques, and fostering a culture of collaboration and accountability, meaningful change becomes possible. The journey toward sustainability is one of continuous learning and adaptation, driven by a shared commitment to creating a healthier and more resilient future for all. Through strategic target-setting and diligent progress measurement, we unlock the potential to transform waste into opportunity and make a lasting positive impact on our world.

Tools and Technologies for Waste Tracking

Waste tracking is integral to effective waste management, providing insights that inform decision-making and drive sustainability initiatives. The tools and technologies available for waste tracking have evolved significantly, offering innovative solutions that streamline data collection and analysis. These advancements empower individuals, businesses, and communities to monitor waste generation, optimize waste reduction strategies, and contribute to a circular economy.

Traditional waste tracking methods often relied on manual data collection, which could be time-consuming and prone to errors. Today, however, digital tools have revolutionized the process, offering greater accuracy and efficiency. One of the most common methods involves using spreadsheets or databases to record waste data. These digital platforms enable the organization and storage of large volumes of data, facilitating easy access and analysis. By creating customized templates, users can track specific waste streams, categorize materials, and calculate quantities, providing a detailed overview of waste generation patterns.

For those seeking to automate and enhance waste tracking, specialized software solutions are available. These programs offer comprehensive features designed to streamline the tracking process, from data entry to reporting. Waste management software often includes modules for tracking waste types, volumes, and disposal methods, as well as tools for generating reports and visualizations. This functionality enables users to identify trends, assess the effectiveness of waste reduction measures, and make informed decisions based on real-time data.

Mobile applications have also emerged as valuable tools for waste tracking, offering flexibility and convenience. These apps allow users to input waste data on-the-go, making it easy to record information directly at the source. Some applications offer additional features, such as barcode scanning or image recognition, to simplify data entry and enhance accuracy. By leveraging mobile technology, users can maintain up-to-date records and access insights from anywhere, supporting dynamic and responsive waste management practices.

IoT (Internet of Things) devices are transforming waste tracking by providing real-time monitoring capabilities. Smart bins equipped with sensors can measure waste levels, detect contamination, and even sort materials automatically. These devices transmit data to central management systems, enabling precise tracking and optimization of waste collection schedules. By reducing the frequency of unnecessary pickups, IoT solutions contribute to cost savings, decreased emissions, and improved operational efficiency.

RFID (Radio-Frequency Identification) technology offers another innovative approach to waste tracking. By attaching RFID tags to waste containers or bins, users can track the movement and disposal of waste throughout its lifecycle. This technology provides detailed information about waste streams, enabling more accurate assessments of waste generation and diversion rates. Additionally, RFID systems can enhance transparency and accountability, ensuring compliance with waste management regulations and standards.

Data analytics and visualization tools play a crucial role in interpreting waste tracking data, transforming raw numbers into actionable insights. Advanced analytics platforms can process large datasets and identify patterns or anomalies, offering predictive insights that drive strategic planning. Visualization tools, such as dashboards or charts, present data in a clear and accessible format, making it easier to communicate findings to stakeholders. These tools enhance decision-making by providing a comprehensive view of waste management performance and highlighting areas for improvement.

Collaboration platforms and cloud-based solutions facilitate the sharing and management of waste tracking data across teams and locations. By providing centralized access to data and resources, these platforms enable seamless collaboration and coordination. Stakeholders can share insights, discuss findings, and develop strategies collectively, fostering a culture of transparency and cooperation. Cloud-based systems also offer scalability and flexibility, accommodating the needs of organizations of all sizes and adapting to changing requirements.

While technology offers significant benefits for waste tracking, successful implementation requires careful planning and consideration. It's essential to select tools and technologies that align with specific goals, resources, and capabilities. Conducting a needs assessment can help identify the most suitable solutions, ensuring that they address key requirements and provide tangible benefits. Training and support are also critical to maximizing the effectiveness of waste tracking technologies, equipping users with the skills and knowledge needed to leverage their full potential.

As waste tracking tools and technologies continue to evolve, they offer unprecedented opportunities to improve waste management practices and achieve sustainability objectives. By embracing these innovations, individuals, businesses, and communities can gain valuable insights into waste generation patterns, optimize resource use, and contribute to a more sustainable future. The power of technology lies in its ability to transform data into action, driving progress and inspiring positive change in waste management systems worldwide. Through the integration of cutting-edge tools and technologies, we can pave the way for a more efficient, transparent, and environmentally responsible approach to waste management.

Chapter 5: Sustainable Practices for Businesses and Industries

Implementing Zero-Waste Policies

Adopting zero-waste policies is a transformative step toward sustainable living, focusing on the efficient use of resources and the elimination of waste. These policies aim to redesign systems and processes to ensure that all products are reused, repaired, or recycled, minimizing the need for landfill disposal. Implementing zero-waste strategies requires a comprehensive approach involving individuals, businesses, and communities working collaboratively to achieve a common goal.

The journey toward zero waste begins with a shift in mindset, embracing the principles of reducing, reusing, and recycling. Reducing consumption is paramount, emphasizing the importance of mindful purchasing and the prioritization of quality over quantity. By selecting durable, long-lasting products and avoiding single-use items, individuals can significantly decrease their waste footprint. Additionally, engaging in thoughtful consumption practices, such as borrowing, renting, or sharing resources, further supports waste reduction efforts.

Reusing items extends their lifecycle, preventing them from becoming waste. This practice can be as simple as repurposing household items, such as using glass jars for storage or cloth bags for shopping. Encouraging creativity and innovation in repurposing can lead to unique and practical solutions that reduce waste. Repairing broken or damaged items instead of discarding them also contributes to waste reduction, fostering a culture of resourcefulness and sustainability.

Recycling remains a crucial component of zero-waste policies, though it should be viewed as a last resort after reducing and reusing. Effective recycling requires a clear understanding of local recycling guidelines, as well as a commitment to sorting and cleaning recyclables properly. Communities can enhance recycling efforts by providing accessible facilities, engaging in public education campaigns, and offering incentives for participation. By improving recycling rates and reducing contamination, the efficiency and impact of recycling programs can be maximized.

Businesses play a significant role in implementing zero-waste policies, as they have the potential to influence supply chains, production processes, and consumer behavior. Developing sustainable business practices involves evaluating and reengineering operations to minimize waste at every stage. For example, adopting lean manufacturing techniques can reduce excess production, while sourcing materials from sustainable suppliers supports circular economy principles. Additionally, businesses can design products with end-of-life considerations in mind, ensuring that they are easily recyclable or compostable.

Packaging represents a major area of concern for businesses striving for zero waste. Transitioning to sustainable packaging options, such as biodegradable materials or reusable containers, can significantly reduce waste. Encouraging customers to return or reuse packaging not only minimizes environmental impact but also fosters brand loyalty and consumer engagement. By prioritizing sustainable packaging solutions, businesses can demonstrate their commitment to sustainability and differentiate themselves in the marketplace.

Community involvement is essential for the successful implementation of zero-waste policies. Local governments and organizations can facilitate community-wide initiatives, such as waste reduction workshops, neighborhood swap events, or composting programs. These initiatives create opportunities for residents to learn, share resources, and collaborate on waste reduction efforts. By fostering a sense of community and shared responsibility, individuals are more likely to embrace zero-waste practices and contribute to collective goals.

Educational institutions also have a vital role in promoting zero waste, serving as both educators and role models for sustainable practices. By integrating zero-waste principles into curricula, schools can raise awareness and equip students with the knowledge and skills needed to make informed choices. Implementing waste reduction programs on campus, such as composting or recycling initiatives, provides students with hands-on experience and inspires them to adopt sustainable habits.

Policy and regulation are powerful tools for driving change and supporting zero-waste initiatives. Governments can enact legislation that encourages waste reduction, such as bans on single-use plastics, incentives for sustainable practices, or requirements for producer responsibility. These policies create a supportive environment for individuals and businesses to pursue zero-waste goals, ensuring that efforts are aligned with broader sustainability objectives.

Monitoring and evaluation are critical components of zero-waste policy implementation, providing insights into progress and areas for improvement. Regular waste audits and data analysis allow stakeholders to assess the effectiveness of strategies and make informed adjustments. By setting clear targets and tracking progress, communities and organizations can maintain momentum and celebrate achievements, reinforcing commitment to zero-waste objectives.

Implementing zero-waste policies is a dynamic and multifaceted endeavor that requires collaboration, innovation, and dedication. By embracing the principles of reducing, reusing, and recycling, individuals, businesses, and communities can work together to create a more sustainable and resilient future. The path to zero waste is both a challenge and an opportunity, offering the potential to transform our relationship with resources and redefine our approach to consumption. Through collective action and commitment, we can pave the way for a world where waste is minimized, resources are valued, and sustainability is at the forefront of our choices.

Green Procurement and Supply Chain Management

Green procurement and supply chain management stand at the forefront of sustainable business practices, offering a strategic approach to reducing environmental impact while enhancing operational efficiency. By integrating environmental considerations into purchasing and supply chain decisions, organizations can drive significant change and promote sustainability across industries. This chapter delves into the principles, practices, and benefits of green procurement and supply chain management, providing a comprehensive guide for businesses seeking to embrace a greener future.

In its essence, green procurement involves selecting products and services that minimize negative environmental and social impacts. This practice extends beyond simple cost considerations, incorporating factors such as resource efficiency, lifecycle impact, and ethical sourcing into purchasing decisions. By prioritizing sustainable options, organizations can reduce their ecological footprint and contribute to a more sustainable economy.

A key aspect of green procurement is understanding the lifecycle of products and services. This involves evaluating the environmental impact of a product from its raw material extraction to its end-of-life disposal. By considering the entire lifecycle, organizations can identify opportunities to minimize waste, energy consumption, and emissions. For example, choosing products made from recycled materials or those that are easily recyclable can significantly reduce environmental impact.

Supplier engagement is crucial to the success of green procurement initiatives. Building strong relationships with suppliers allows organizations to collaborate on sustainability goals and encourage the adoption of environmentally friendly practices. This might involve working with suppliers to develop sustainable product lines, improve resource efficiency, or implement waste reduction measures. Transparent communication and shared objectives foster a culture of sustainability throughout the supply chain.

Establishing clear criteria and standards for green procurement is essential for guiding purchasing decisions. These criteria might include certifications such as Energy Star, Fair Trade, or Forest Stewardship Council (FSC) labels, which indicate compliance with specific environmental or social standards. By adhering to established criteria, organizations can ensure consistency and accountability in their procurement processes, reinforcing their commitment to sustainability.

Supply chain management plays a pivotal role in green procurement, as it encompasses the coordination and oversight of all activities involved in the production, transportation, and delivery of goods and services. Sustainable supply chain management focuses on optimizing these activities to reduce environmental impact while maintaining efficiency and cost-effectiveness. This involves rethinking logistics, material sourcing, and production processes to incorporate sustainability at every stage.

One effective strategy in sustainable supply chain management is to localize production and sourcing. By prioritizing local suppliers and manufacturers, organizations can reduce transportation distances, lowering greenhouse gas emissions and transportation costs. Local sourcing also supports regional economies and communities, fostering stronger relationships and collaboration between businesses and suppliers.

Another approach is to implement circular economy principles within the supply chain. This involves designing products and processes with the goal of keeping resources in use for as long as possible, extracting maximum value before recovery and regeneration. Circular supply chains focus on minimizing waste through recycling, reusing, and remanufacturing, ultimately reducing the need for virgin materials and decreasing overall environmental impact.

Technology and data analytics play a significant role in advancing green procurement and supply chain management. Digital tools enable real-time monitoring and analysis of supply chain activities, providing insights into resource consumption, emissions, and waste generation. This information empowers organizations to identify inefficiencies, optimize processes, and make informed decisions that support sustainability objectives. Technologies such as blockchain can enhance transparency and traceability, ensuring accountability and trust throughout the supply chain.

While the benefits of green procurement and supply chain management are substantial, implementing these practices requires careful planning and commitment. Organizations must invest in training and education to equip employees with the knowledge and skills needed to navigate sustainability challenges. This includes understanding environmental standards, evaluating product certifications, and developing relationships with suppliers who share sustainability values.

Collaboration and partnerships are also essential for driving progress in green procurement and sustainable supply chain management. By working with industry peers, government agencies, and non-governmental organizations, businesses can share best practices, leverage resources, and advocate for policies that support sustainability. Collective action amplifies the impact of individual efforts, accelerating the transition toward a more sustainable future.

Ultimately, green procurement and supply chain management represent a powerful opportunity for organizations to align their operations with sustainability principles. By embracing these practices, businesses can reduce their environmental footprint, enhance their reputation, and drive innovation in product and service offerings. As the global focus on sustainability intensifies, organizations that prioritize green procurement and supply chain management will be well-positioned to thrive in a rapidly evolving marketplace, contributing to a healthier planet and a more sustainable economy for generations to come.

Waste Reduction in Manufacturing and Production

Manufacturing and production processes are significant contributors to waste generation, making them prime targets for waste reduction efforts. The drive for efficiency and sustainability in these sectors is more critical than ever, as industries aim to balance economic growth with environmental responsibility. By adopting innovative strategies and technologies, manufacturers can reduce waste, optimize resource use, and enhance their competitive advantage.

The first step in reducing waste in manufacturing is conducting a comprehensive analysis of current processes and practices. This involves examining every stage of production, from raw material acquisition to product delivery, to identify inefficiencies and waste streams. Gathering data on material usage, energy consumption, and waste outputs provides a clear picture of the areas that require attention. By understanding these dynamics, manufacturers can devise targeted strategies to minimize waste and improve overall efficiency.

Lean manufacturing principles offer a framework for reducing waste and enhancing productivity. By focusing on value creation and the elimination of non-value-added activities, lean practices streamline operations and reduce resource consumption. Techniques such as just-in-time production, which synchronizes production schedules with demand, minimize overproduction and excess inventory. Additionally, implementing continuous improvement methodologies, such as Six Sigma, fosters a culture of innovation and problem-solving, driving incremental advancements in waste reduction.

The adoption of circular economy principles represents a paradigm shift in manufacturing, emphasizing the need to design products and processes that prioritize resource efficiency and waste minimization. This approach involves rethinking product design to facilitate disassembly, repair, and recycling, ultimately extending product lifecycles and reducing the need for virgin materials. By incorporating recycled content into new products and establishing take-back programs for end-of-life products, manufacturers can create closed-loop systems that significantly reduce waste.

Material efficiency is another crucial aspect of waste reduction in manufacturing. Opting for sustainable and renewable materials, as well as minimizing material waste through precision cutting and advanced manufacturing techniques, can lead to substantial reductions in waste. Technologies such as 3D printing allow for the creation of complex components with minimal material waste, offering opportunities for customization and innovation. By optimizing material use, manufacturers can reduce costs while contributing to environmental sustainability.

Energy efficiency plays a vital role in waste reduction, as energy consumption is closely linked to emissions and other environmental impacts. Implementing energy-saving technologies, such as high-efficiency motors, LED lighting, and advanced heating and cooling systems, can significantly reduce energy waste. Additionally, integrating renewable energy sources, such as solar or wind power, into manufacturing operations reduces reliance on fossil fuels and lowers the carbon footprint of production processes.

Water management is another critical consideration in waste reduction, particularly in industries with high water usage. Implementing water recycling and reuse systems can minimize water waste, reduce costs, and alleviate pressure on local water resources. By monitoring water use and identifying leaks or inefficiencies, manufacturers can optimize water management and contribute to sustainable water stewardship.

Waste reduction efforts in manufacturing also extend to supply chain management, as the interconnected nature of supply chains means that waste generated by suppliers can impact overall efficiency. Collaborating with suppliers to implement sustainable practices, such as reducing packaging or optimizing transportation routes, can lead to significant waste reductions. Establishing partnerships with suppliers who share sustainability goals fosters a culture of collaboration and shared responsibility throughout the supply chain.

Employee engagement is a critical component of successful waste reduction initiatives. By fostering a culture of sustainability and empowering employees to contribute ideas and solutions, manufacturers can harness the creativity and expertise of their workforce. Training programs that raise awareness of waste reduction practices and encourage sustainable behaviors enhance employee buy-in and drive collective action toward sustainability goals.

Technology and data analytics are powerful tools for identifying waste reduction opportunities and optimizing manufacturing processes. Advanced sensors and monitoring systems provide real-time data on production efficiency, energy use, and waste generation, enabling manufacturers to make informed decisions and quickly address issues. Data analytics platforms facilitate the analysis of large datasets, uncovering patterns and insights that drive strategic planning and continuous improvement.

As manufacturers pursue waste reduction, setting clear goals and measuring progress are essential to maintaining momentum and ensuring accountability. Establishing key performance indicators and regularly reviewing performance data provide a framework for evaluating success and identifying areas for further improvement. Celebrating achievements and sharing success stories reinforce commitment to sustainability and inspire ongoing efforts.

In conclusion, waste reduction in manufacturing and production is a multifaceted endeavor that requires a holistic approach, innovative thinking, and a commitment to sustainability. By embracing lean and circular economy principles, optimizing resource use, and leveraging technology, manufacturers can achieve significant waste reductions while enhancing efficiency and competitiveness. The transition to sustainable manufacturing is both a challenge and an opportunity, offering the potential to create a more resilient and environmentally responsible future for industries and communities worldwide. Through collaboration, innovation, and continuous improvement, manufacturers can lead the way in transforming production practices and contributing to a sustainable global economy.

Employee Engagement and Training Programs

Employee engagement and training programs are pivotal in fostering a sustainable workplace culture where waste reduction and environmental responsibility are second nature. By equipping employees with the skills and motivation to embrace sustainable practices, organizations can harness the collective power of their workforce to drive meaningful change. This chapter delves into effective strategies for engaging employees and implementing training programs that inspire and empower teams to contribute to sustainability goals.

Creating a culture of sustainability begins with leadership commitment. When leaders demonstrate a genuine commitment to environmental initiatives, it sets a powerful example that resonates throughout the organization. Leaders can cultivate this culture by integrating sustainability into the company's core values, mission, and strategic objectives. By consistently communicating the importance of sustainability and aligning it with the organization's vision, leaders inspire employees to prioritize environmental considerations in their daily work.

To truly engage employees, it's essential to involve them in the development and implementation of sustainability initiatives. Encouraging participation in brainstorming sessions, working groups, or sustainability committees allows employees to voice their ideas and insights, fostering a sense of ownership and investment in the outcomes. This collaborative approach not only generates innovative solutions but also enhances employee satisfaction and morale by demonstrating that their contributions are valued.

Effective communication is key to maintaining engagement and ensuring that sustainability remains a priority. Regular updates on progress, successes, and challenges keep employees informed and motivated. Utilizing a variety of communication channels, such as newsletters, emails, or intranet portals, ensures that messages reach all employees, regardless of their location or role. Celebrating achievements, whether big or small, reinforces positive behaviors and encourages continued efforts toward sustainability goals.

Training programs are a cornerstone of successful employee engagement in sustainability initiatives. These programs should be tailored to meet the specific needs and roles of employees, ensuring that they are relevant, practical, and impactful. For example, training for facilities staff might focus on energy efficiency and waste management techniques, while office staff training might emphasize paper reduction and digital tools. By providing targeted training, organizations empower employees with the knowledge and skills needed to make informed and sustainable choices.

Interactive and hands-on training methods enhance learning and retention, making sustainability concepts more relatable and actionable. Workshops, simulations, or role-playing exercises can engage employees in real-world scenarios, allowing them to practice sustainability skills in a supportive environment. Additionally, incorporating storytelling or case studies into training sessions can illustrate the tangible benefits of sustainable practices, inspiring employees to adopt these behaviors in their own work.

Mentorship and peer-to-peer learning are valuable components of employee engagement and training programs. Pairing employees with sustainability champions or mentors within the organization fosters knowledge sharing and accelerates the adoption of sustainable practices. Peer-to-peer learning encourages collaboration and camaraderie, creating a supportive network that reinforces the organization's sustainability objectives. By leveraging the expertise and enthusiasm of sustainability advocates, organizations can inspire a wider cultural shift toward environmental responsibility.

Gamification is another innovative approach to engaging employees in sustainability initiatives. By incorporating game-like elements, such as challenges, competitions, or rewards, organizations can make sustainability efforts more engaging and enjoyable. For example, a company might host a waste reduction challenge where departments compete to achieve the greatest reduction in waste over a set period. Participants can earn points, badges, or recognition for their efforts, adding a sense of fun and motivation to the process.

Feedback and recognition are powerful motivators for sustaining employee engagement in sustainability initiatives. Providing regular feedback on performance and acknowledging contributions reinforces positive behaviors and encourages ongoing participation. Recognition can take many forms, from formal awards or certificates to informal shout-outs during team meetings. By celebrating individual and team achievements, organizations demonstrate their appreciation for employees' efforts and reinforce the collective commitment to sustainability.

Continuous improvement is essential for maintaining momentum and ensuring the long-term success of employee engagement and training programs. Organizations should regularly assess the effectiveness of their programs, soliciting feedback from participants and identifying areas for enhancement. By adapting training content, methods, or delivery based on feedback and changing needs, organizations can keep programs fresh, relevant, and impactful.

Employee engagement and training programs are not only about imparting knowledge and skills but also about inspiring a shared commitment to sustainability. When employees understand the impact of their actions and feel empowered to contribute to environmental goals, they become passionate advocates for change. Through collaboration, innovation, and dedication, organizations can create a workplace culture where sustainability is embedded in every aspect of operations, driving progress toward a more sustainable future for all.